W9-CGW-998

EXPLORERS!

Henry Hudson

Explorer of the Hudson River

Arlene Bourgeois Molzahn

Enslow Publishers, Inc.

40 Industrial Road   PO Box 38
Box 398   Aldershot
Berkeley Heights, NJ 07922   Hants GU12 6BP
USA   UK

http://www.enslow.com

With love to Peter who has made my being a grandmother so very special.

Library of Congress Cataloging-in-Publication Data

Molzahn, Arlene Bourgeois.
    Henry Hudson : explorer of the Hudson River / Arlene Bourgeois Molzahn.
        p. cm. — (Explorers!)
    Summary: Discusses the life of Henry Hudson, the English sea captain who explored the Arctic Ocean and the river and bay later named for him while in search of a northern route to the Indies.
    Includes bibliographical references and index.
    ISBN-10: 0-7660-2070-3
    1. Hudson, Henry, d. 1611—Juvenile literature. 2. Explorers—America—Biography—Juvenile literature. 3. Explorers—Great Britain—Biography—Juvenile literature. 4. America—Discovery and exploration—English—Juvenile literature. 5. Hudson River Valley (N.Y. and N.J.)—Discovery and exploration—Juvenile literature.
[1. Hudson, Henry, d. 1611. 2. Explorers. 3. America—Discovery and exploration—English.] I. Title. II. Series: Explorers! (Enslow Publishers)
E129.H8 M65 2003
910'.92—dc21   2002012807

ISBN-13: 978-0-7660-2070-2

Printed in the United States of America

10 9 8 7 6 5 4 3

To Our Readers: We have done our best to make sure all Internet Addresses in this book were active and appropriate when we went to press. However, the author and the publisher have no control over and assume no liability for the material available on those Internet sites or on other Web sites they may link to. Any comments or suggestions can be sent by e-mail to comments@enslow.com or to the address on the back cover.

Illustration on page 1: This is Henry Hudson's *Half Moon* in 1609.

Please note: Compasses on the cover and in the book are from © 1999 Artville, LLC.

All Journal Entries are from *Henry Hudson, The Navigator*, printed for the Hakluyt Society, M.DCCC.LX; illustrations within the Journal Entry box are from the Library of Congress, pp. 16, 27, 38. Spelling and punctuation are as in journal.

Contents

List of Maps

North Pole

Greenland

Iceland

Norway

England

Holland

North

America

N
W   E
S

Henry Hudson went on four voyages
between 1607 and 1611. He sailed to
places like Greenland and North
America.

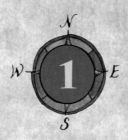

Exciting Times

The 1400s to the 1800s were considered the Age of Exploration. Many great discoveries were being made at this time. Explorers like Christopher Columbus and Ferdinand Magellan had sailed the seas. In 1492, Columbus made his first voyage and found lands in the Caribbean Sea. In 1519, Magellan started his voyage. He was the first to lead a voyage around the world.

In Europe at this time, many men were searching for a way to get to the Indies by crossing the oceans. Reaching the Indies would mean the men and their country would become very rich.

Henry Hudson probably heard stories about these explorers. He might have dreamed about one day sailing on a ship. We do not know much about Hudson's life, but we do know about his exciting discoveries.

Henry Hudson was born

Christopher Columbus set sail in 1492 and discovered lands in the Caribbean Sea.

In 1519, Ferdinand Magellan was the first European to lead an expedition around the world. While he did not finish his voyage, his men did.

in England, but no one knows on what day or year he was born.

Hudson must have gone to school because he could read and write. Most schools in those days were only for boys. They were taught reading, writing, mathematics, history, geography, and Latin and Greek.

Hudson had a wife named Katherine, and three sons, John, Oliver, and Richard.

During this time, Spain and Portugal controlled the water routes around the coast of Africa. They did not let ships from other European countries reach the Indies. So people were trying to find a different way to the Indies.

Most schools during Henry Hudson's time were only for boys. A page from a 1545 book shows the Sun and planets.

The Indies

The countries of India, China, Japan, and the East Indies were known as the Indies. At this time, there were no refrigerators. Spices like cloves, cinnamon, nutmeg, and pepper were used to cover up the taste of spoiled foods.

Traders wanted to reach the Indies to trade for silks and spices. There was already a land route from Europe to the Indies. Spices and silk goods were brought by boat over the Red Sea. Then the goods were loaded on camel caravans that brought them to Europe. This route was dangerous. Traders from Europe were not wanted on the route. People wanted to find a new and safer route to the Indies.

During this time, many people were searching for the Indies. Many thought the Indies were the countries of India, China, and Japan. This is what they look like today.

The Muscovy Company was a group of English merchants. They were looking for a northern water route to the Indies. Some people believed that ships from Europe could sail across the North Pole to reach the Indies. They knew that the sun shines for twenty-four hours in the summer at the North Pole. They thought the waters at the North Pole would not be frozen during the summer.

Hudson probably went to sea as a young man and learned how to sail a ship. In 1607, the Muscovy Company hired him as a captain to find a route to the Indies by sailing across the North Pole.

Tailors shops in the sixteenth century looked like this. Silk goods were brought to the shops from the Indies.

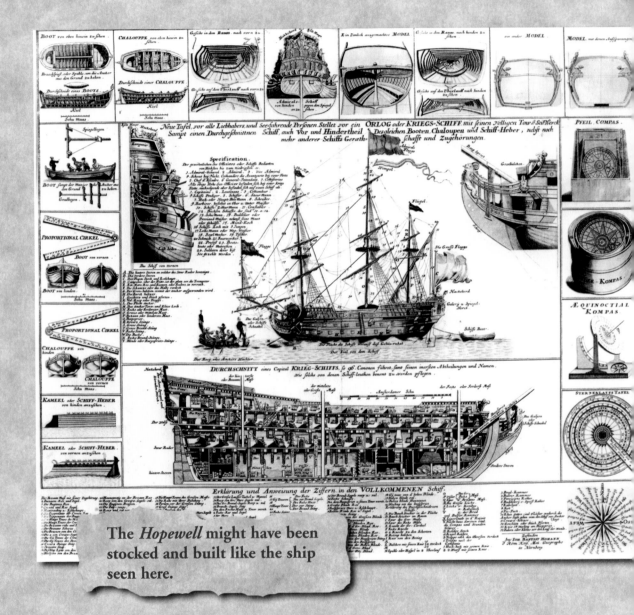

The *Hopewell* might have been stocked and built like the ship seen here.

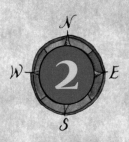

Near the North Pole

The men of the Muscovy Company believed that a ship could sail north across the North Pole and then sail south to the Indies. The company bought a three-mast sailing ship named the *Hopewell*. The *Hopewell* was a small wooden ship that had sailed on six other voyages. Henry Hudson was chosen as captain. His job was to find a way to reach the Indies by sailing across the waters of the North Pole.

Hudson stocked the Hopewell with dried beef, pickled pork, dried peas, carrots, onions, salt, and barley flour. Hudson also had to take fresh water for the trip.

Henry Hudson packed plenty of food for the crew, but planned to catch fish as well.

He planned to have the crew catch fish. Some of the fish would be used for food. The rest of the fish would be salted and brought back to England to be sold.

Ten men were chosen to sail with Hudson. The eleventh member of the crew was Hudson's middle son, John.

On April 23, 1607, Hudson and his crew set sail from London to begin the voyage to the North Pole. On June 13, the men on the *Hopewell* spotted the island of Greenland. Hudson believed that Greenland was just a small island. He sailed along the coast. He tried to find a passage through the island. He kept notes and made charts of the Greenland coast. Most maps of the 1600s showed Greenland as the western part of Norway. Other maps showed Greenland separated from Norway by only a few miles of open water. Hudson sailed north believing that he would find a new route to the Indies.

As they sailed around Greenland, the men saw seals and walruses. By the end of June, the *Hopewell* had reached a group of islands called Spitsbergen. Icy winds

In the 1600s, many maps showed Norway and Greenland as one. Here is the coast of Norway.

Northwest Passage and Northeast Passage

Explorers during this time thought a Northwest Passage, or waterway, would lead them across or around North America. A Northeast Passage would lead them across or around Europe and Asia. Many tried to find such a passage. In 1524, Giovanni da Verrazano searched as far as Maine for the waterway. Then in 1535, another explorer, Jacque Cartier, tried to find the Northwest Passage, and found the St. Lawrence River. Even after Henry Hudson tried to find the passage in the early 1600s, many explorers continued the search.

Through the years, explorers made great discoveries. In 1906, Roald Amundsen completed the first west-to-east voyage through the Northwest Passage. Amundsen also sailed the Northeast Passage.

Here is a map of Greenland from the late 1600s. On Hudson's first voyage, he sailed along the coast.

and freezing temperatures made it impossible to continue sailing. Hudson anchored the ship in a small bay along the coast of one of the islands. As soon as the weather improved, the men of the *Hopewell* started making repairs to the ship's torn sails.

When the ship was repaired, the *Hopewell* sailed along the coast of the islands of Spitsbergen. On July 14, 1607,

Many explorers at this time used the stars in the night sky to figure out what direction they were headed.

From the Journal of Henry Hudson

"In this bay we saw many whales, and one of our company having a hooke and line over-boord to trie for fish, a whale came under the keele of our ship and made her held . . ."

Hudson sailed his ship into a quiet bay. The bay was full of hundreds of large whales. It was later called Whales Bay.

Two days later, the *Hopewell* was about 575 miles from the North Pole. Water began to freeze around the ship. Hudson realized that he could no longer travel north. He decided to return to England.

Whales and Ice

The *Hopewell* reached England on September 15, 1607. Henry Hudson gave his report to the Muscovy Company. He told the merchants that he did not find a route to the Indies. But Hudson told them about the whales he had seen in Whales Bay. The Muscovy Company quickly made plans to hunt the whales.

At that time, whales were very valuable. Many parts of the whale could be used. Whale blubber was cooked to make oil. The oil was burned in lamps. Baleen was used to make women's corsets, dress hoops, and whips.

A substance called ambergris is found in whales. It is

During Henry Hudson's day, whales were very valuable. All parts of the whales were used.

used in making perfumes. Ambergris was worth more money than spices from the Indies.

Because of the discovery of Whales Bay, many other companies tried to hire Hudson. They wanted him to guide them to Whales Bay. But Hudson did not want to take part in hunting whales. All he wanted was to find another route to the Indies.

By 1608, Henry Hudson was known all over Europe. His discovery of the whales had made the Muscovy Company very rich. Companies from other countries hurried to Whales Bay. They were also getting rich by hunting the whales.

Since his first voyage was a success, Hudson wanted

to sail again. He asked the Muscovy Company for a second chance to find the Indies. Hudson wanted to try sailing toward the North Pole again. The Muscovy Company gave him the money for the trip.

The hull of the *Hopewell* was made stronger so that it would be safer going through icy waters. Hudson bought food supplies and hired new sailors for the trip. The ship had a crew of fourteen, including Hudson's son John. Hudson was a bad judge of men. Some of the sailors he hired were troublemakers.

Hudson left London, England, on April 22, 1608.

After Hudson's discovery of Whales Bay, many companies started hunting the whales.

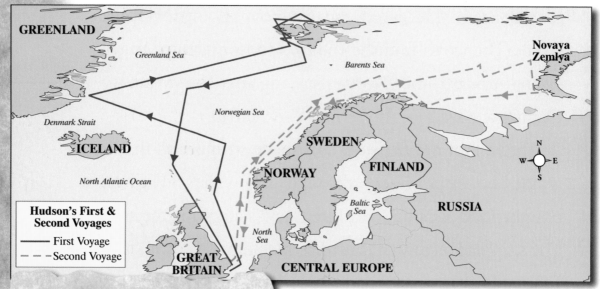

This map shows Hudson's first and second voyages. He was trying to find the Northwest Passage.

The beginning of the voyage went well. But by the middle of June, ice floes could be seen in the water. Hudson continued sailing north and east until he reached Novaya Zemlya, a group of islands north of Norway. Hudson sailed along the coast and made maps of the islands.

On July 6, 1608, Hudson and his crew could no longer travel north because of the ice. The *Hopewell* turned back, but it did not sail back toward England. Instead, Hudson began sailing west. He hoped to find the Northwest Passage.

After a few days of sailing west, the crew became angry. The crew was ready to take over the ship. When sailors threaten to take over a ship, it is called mutiny. They met with Hudson. The crew wanted the ship to sail back to England. Hudson did not want mutiny. So he sailed back to England without finding the Northwest Passage.

On August 26, 1608, the *Hopewell* returned to England.

To avoid a mutiny, Henry Hudson gave up on looking for the Northwest Passage and returned to England.

For Henry Hudson's third voyage, the Dutch East India Company gave him the *Half Moon*. Hudson and his crew left Amsterdam, Holland, in April 1609.

Sailing for Holland

The Muscovy Company felt that Hudson's second voyage had been a failure. They told him he no longer had a job with the company. He had very little to show for his first two voyages. And he still had not found a new water route to the Indies.

Some people from Holland were also searching for the Northwest and Northeast Passages. Merchants of the Dutch East India Company met with Hudson. But they did not know if they wanted Henry Hudson sailing for them. When the French became interested in Hudson, the Dutch quickly hired him to find a route to the Indies.

This is what a house and windmill in the Netherlands might look like today. Holland is part of the Netherlands.

The Dutch East India Company gave Henry Hudson the ship *Halve Maen* for his third voyage. *Halve Maen* is "half moon" in Dutch. This ship was in very poor shape. Twenty sailors were chosen for the voyage. John Hudson was part of the crew again.

The crew of the *Half Moon* was made up of English sailors who spoke only English, and Dutch sailors who spoke only Dutch. The crew was divided into two groups. The sailors from the two countries could not understand each other. Hudson himself did not speak Dutch. This caused some very difficult times on the ship.

The *Half Moon* left Amsterdam, Holland, on April 6, 1609. It headed north for the coast of Norway. By the

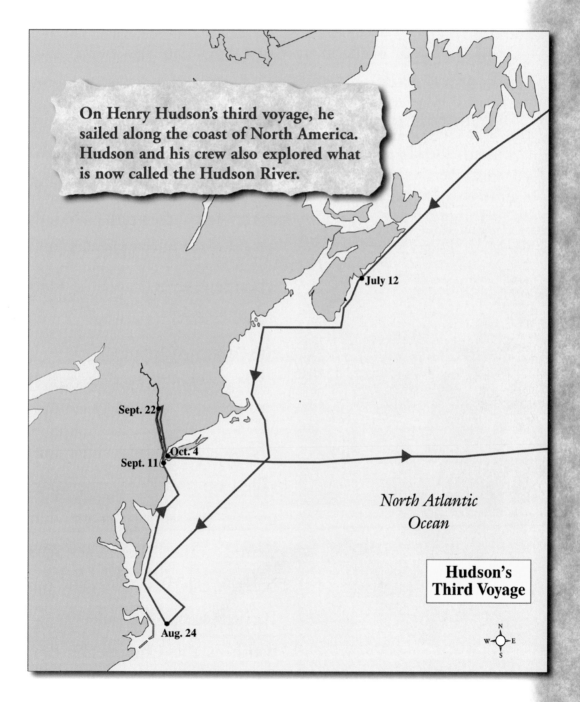

On Henry Hudson's third voyage, he sailed along the coast of North America. Hudson and his crew also explored what is now called the Hudson River.

July 12

Sept. 22

Oct. 4

Sept. 11

North Atlantic Ocean

Hudson's Third Voyage

Aug. 24

N
W · E
S

middle of May it had reached the same icy waters that had forced Hudson to turn back on his other two voyages. The crew was getting angry. There was talk of mutiny. Hudson gave the crew a choice. He said that the ship should start sailing west. He told them he had heard about a Northwest Passage that led through North America to the Pacific Ocean. The crew agreed and the *Half Moon* started its voyage across the Atlantic Ocean.

Henry Hudson wanted to find the Northwest Passage.

The *Half Moon* reached North America during the first week of July. The ship sailed up and down the coast trying to find a river that would take them to the Northwest Passage and the Pacific Ocean. He sailed as far south as the Chesapeake Bay, in the present day states of

Maryland and Virginia. On September 3, 1609, the ship sailed into what is now New York Harbor. While exploring the harbor, Hudson and his crew saw American Indians.

Hudson sailed the *Half Moon* 150 miles up the river that later was named for him. This river is the

From the Journal of
Robert Jeut
(crewman with Henry Hudson)

This day the people of the countrey came abord of us, seeming very glad of our coming, and brought greene tobacco, and gave us of it for knives and beads. They goe in deere skins loose, well dressed. . . . They desire cloathes, and are very civill.

As Henry Hudson sailed into what is now New York Harbor, Indians watched from the shore.

Henry Hudson thought the river that was later named for him would lead to the Pacific Ocean.

Hudson and his crew met Indians that lived along the Hudson River.

Hudson River. He claimed the land for the Dutch. He believed that this river would take him to the Pacific Ocean, but he was wrong.

Hudson called his crew together. He told them that it would soon be winter. The men were given a choice. They could stay in these new lands for the winter, or they could sail back to Europe. The men chose to return to their homes in England and Holland.

On November 7, 1609, the *Half Moon* reached England. Henry Hudson's third voyage had ended.

King James I of England arrested Henry Hudson because Hudson had sailed for Holland and not England.

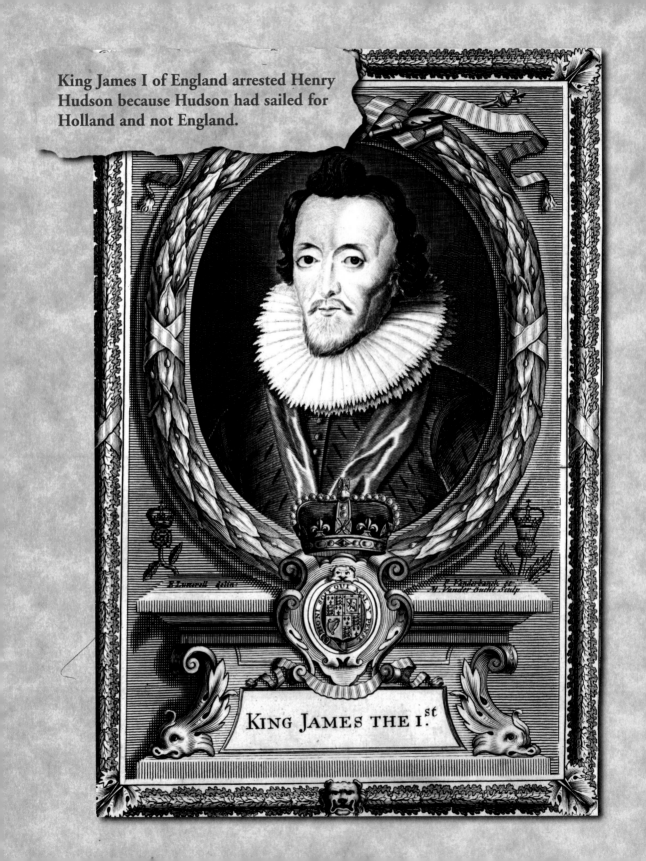

KING JAMES THE 1st

Long Winter

King James I of England was very angry with Hudson because he had sailed for Holland. As soon as the *Half Moon* docked in England, King James put Hudson under house arrest. He was not put in prison, but officers followed him all the time. He could not leave England without the king's permission. The Dutch sailors returned the *Half Moon* to Holland without Hudson.

Hudson did not like being under house arrest. He was afraid the king would not let him sail again. He talked to a group of English merchants and to the king's son, Henry. He told them that the Northwest Passage could

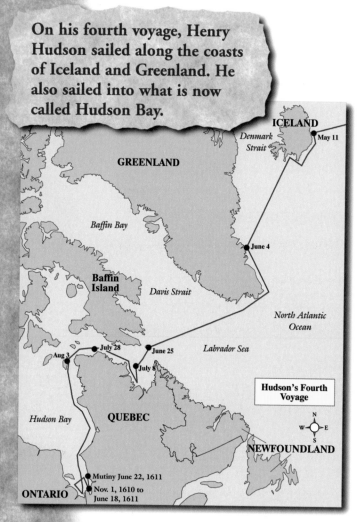

On his fourth voyage, Henry Hudson sailed along the coasts of Iceland and Greenland. He also sailed into what is now called Hudson Bay.

be found. They talked to King James. Finally the king let Hudson sail again but only if he sailed for England.

Hudson was given the ship *Discovery* for his fourth voyage. The *Discovery* was a very good ship. The hull of the ship was built strong enough to sail through icy water. With this ship, Hudson could search for the Northwest Passage.

On April 17, 1610, Hudson set sail from England for the last time. He had a crew of twenty-two sailors. Hudson's son John was a part of the crew again. Also sailing with Hudson again was Robert Juet. Hudson had hired Juet for his last two voyages. Juet had been a troublemaker on both of those trips, but Hudson still hired him for this one.

During the first week in June, the ship passed Greenland. On August 3, 1610, it reached a narrow passage leading inland along the coast of North America. This passage became known as the Hudson Strait. Some of the men took the ship's small boat and went ashore. They climbed a cliff and saw a huge body of water. Hudson thought this was the Pacific Ocean.

During the months of September and October, the

The ship *Discovery*, with Hudson and his crew, sailed past Greenland and reached a narrow passage along the coast of North America. This passage became known as the Hudson Strait.

ship sailed along the coast of what today is called James Bay. This bay is the southern part of Hudson Bay in northeast Canada. Hudson Bay was named for Henry Hudson. By November 10, 1610, the *Discovery* could no longer move. It was frozen in the ice.

It was a long hard winter for the crew. Some of the men stayed on the *Discovery*. Others went ashore and built shelters to live in for the winter.

Food ran out, and the men ate moss that they found under the snow. They all suffered from scurvy. Scurvy is

Henry Hudson and his men thought they had found the Pacific Ocean.

caused from not getting enough vitamin C. Vitamin C is found in fresh fruits and vegetables.

Some of the men suffered from frostbite on their hands and toes. One man froze to death while on a hunting trip.

The men seemed always to be arguing and fighting. Fights were very common. The crew was split into two groups. One group was led by Robert Juet. They blamed all their troubles on Hudson. The other group was loyal to Hudson.

For seven and a half months the *Discovery* was unable to sail. Finally, on June 12, 1611, the weather improved and the *Discovery* could sail again.

The men suffered a long, hard winter. Many suffered from scurvy, which is caused by not getting enough vitamin C. Lemons have vitamin C.

Henry Hudson with his son John, and a few others, were set afloat after his crew started a mutiny.

Mutiny at Sea

The crew wanted to return to England after the winter. But Hudson wanted to continue to search for the Northwest Passage. On June 20, 1611, the *Discovery* sailed from James Bay into Hudson Bay. Hudson thought it was the Northwest Passage. He ordered the men to sail west. This made most of the men very angry. They wanted to return to their homes.

During the night of June 21, Juet and several other men made plans to take over the ship and return to England. They gave the rest of the men a choice. They could side with Hudson, and be set out to sea in a small

From the Journal of
Abacuk Prickett
(crewman with Henry Hudson)

Being thus in ice on Saturday, the one and twentieth of June, at night, Wilson the boatswayne, and Henry Greene, came to mee lying (in my cabbin) lame, and told mee that they and the rest of their associates would shift the company, and turne the master and all the sicke men into the shallop, and let them shift for themselves. Henrie Greene and another went to the carpenter, and held him with a talke till the master [Henry Hudson] came out of his cabbin (which hee soone did); then came John Thomas and Bennet before him, while Wilson bound his armes behind him. He asked them what they meant? They told him he should know when he was in the shallop.

boat. Or, they could stay on the *Discovery* and return to England.

On the morning of June 22, 1611, Hudson and his son John were forced into a small boat. Four men who were sick and three men who decided to stay with

Hudson were also put on the boat. Then it was lowered into the icy cold water. Hudson and the other men who were with him in the boat were never heard from again. The fifteen remaining members of the crew turned the *Discovery* toward England.

The ship reached London, England, on October 20, 1611. Only nine men were left on board. Juet and five others died on the return voyage.

The High Court in London soon found out what happened. The punishment for mutiny was death. This meant the men who returned with the *Discovery* should have been hanged. But these men were clever.

The men showed the

Henry Hudson, his son, and others were forced into a small boat. The *Discovery* sailed back to England.

court maps and charts that belonged to Henry Hudson. The maps showed that there was open sea just beyond where the ship had sailed. The men told the court that this proved that the Northwest Passage had been found. Now these men became very valuable. They had sailed with Hudson and said they knew exactly how to reach the Northwest Passage. Even though the men had been part of a mutiny, they were not hanged. Instead, some men returned to North America for another voyage. Others were able to return to their homes.

What Happened to Henry Hudson?

There are many different stories about what may have happened to Henry Hudson. One story tells about the letters "HH" carved in rocks on the banks of the Ottawa River in Canada. Some people believe Hudson made this carving to let the world know he had reached land. Other stories claim that the markings were made by people who lived in the area. There is another story that people of the area found a boat with a boy who was still alive. He may have been John Hudson.

Some people believe that Henry
Hudson and his men survived the
icy waters and made it to land.

Henry Hudson was a great sailor and a great explorer. He discovered and explored the Hudson River, Hudson Strait, and Hudson Bay. He mapped the Arctic waters for other explorers. His explorations led the Dutch and English to claim land in North America.

Hudson's four voyages brought much information about North America to the people of Europe. This information helped many other adventurers explore the world.

The Hudson River is a major waterway. The river empties into the Atlantic Ocean at New York City, seen here.

Timeline

1565–1575—Henry Hudson was born sometime between these years.

April 23, 1607—Leaves on his first voyage in search of a new route to the Indies on the ship *Hopewell*.

July 14, 1607—Discovers Whales Bay.

September 15, 1607—Returns to England.

April 22, 1608—Begins his second voyage on the *Hopewell*.

August 26, 1608—Returns to England from his second voyage.

April 6, 1609—Sets sail for his third voyage on the *Half Moon*.

July 1609—*Half Moon* reaches the continent of North America.

November 7, 1609—*Half Moon* returns to England.

April 17, 1610—Sets sail on the *Discovery* for his last voyage.

June 22, 1611—Mutiny on the *Discovery*; Hudson and eight other men are set out to sea in a small boat never to be heard from again.

October 20, 1611—*Discovery* returns to England.

Words to Know

ambergris—A substance found in whales used for making perfume.

baleen—A horny substance found in the upper jaws of baleen whales.

blubber—The fat of whales that can be used to make oil.

corset—A tight-fitting article of clothing worn by women under a dress.

continent—A very large body of land. The continents of the world are Asia, Africa, Europe, North America, South America, Antarctica, and Australia.

floe—A sheet of floating ice.

hull—The body or the frame of a ship.

route—A road or a way that people travel.

Learn More About
Henry Hudson

Books

Hurwicz, Claude. *Henry Hudson*. New York: PowerKids Press, 2001.

Saffer, Barbara. *Henry Hudson: Ill-Fated Explorer of North America's Coast*. Philadelphia, Penn.: Chelsea House, 2001.

Santella, Andrew. *Henry Hudson*. New York: Franklin Watts, 2001.

Internet Addresses

The *Half Moon*

<http://www.hudsonriver.com/history/halfmoon.htm>

Find out more about Henry Hudson's ship, Half Moon.

Henry Hudson: Explorer

<http://www.enchantedlearning.com/explorers/page/h/hudson.shtml>

Read more about Henry Hudson and other explorers from this Enchanted Learning Web site.

Index